UNDERSTANDING

CREATION

UNDERSTANDING CREATION

A Concise Biblical Doctrine of Creation

Copyright © 2016. All rights reserved.

No part of this publication may be reproduced, stored in a retrieval system or transmitted in any way by any means, electronic, mechanical, photocopy, recording or otherwise, without the prior permission of the author except as provided by USA copyright law.

All characters appearing in this work are fictitious. Any resemblance to real persons, living or dead, is purely coincidental.

The opinions expressed by the author are not necessarily those of Revival Waves of Glory Books & Publishing.

Published by Revival Waves of Glory Books & Publishing

PO Box 5961 Litchfield, Illinois 62056 USA

www.revivalwavesofgloryministries.com

Revival Waves of Glory Books & Publishing is committed to excellence in the publishing industry.

Book design Copyright © 2016 by Revival Waves of Glory Books & Publishing. All rights reserved.

Published in the United States of America

Paperback: 978-1-68411-216-6

Contents

Introduction iv

CHAPTER ONE: Automatic Creation 1

CHAPTER TWO: Chaos Or Original State Of Earth At Creation? Vs 2 14

CHAPTER THREE: Process Creation: Creation Days – Vs. 3 20

CHAPTER FOUR: Summing Up On The First Three Chapters 25

CHAPTER FIVE: Creation Accounts 31

NOTES 39

Other Books By AUDU SUYUM 42

That this book, Genesis, is old in sense of age is true; but that its message is outdated and therefore irrelevant is a modern pride (Prov. 30:12-13) and confusion.

A Christian who holds to this view and cares not to read and meditate on this book has forgotten his true origin, identity and given away his faith. Such a person has lost sight of life, its journey, and so is unfaithful whatsoever. To be a full person with full right and liberty (patriotic citizen) is to know your origin and maintain your identity. To be faithful is to hold tenably to the matters of faith.

Genesis is a book rich in both history and theology. It tells us the origin of creation, man and marriage, civilization, sin and redemption. God is the originator of all. Man is neither an evolutionary being nor a biological product of reproduction of sexual and asexual union. Life does not originate and spring up from the genetic cells but from God and for him (Acts 17:28). Man is a special creation of God created for a divine purpose and glory. The biological origin of man is an ordained means of bringing into this physical existence an already existed individual whose life and seed are preserved in the sexual organs of the human reproductive system.

There is a God who out of His sovereign will and wisdom decided to produce this world for his good pleasures and governs the creation and the course of every event in love and holiness to the ultimate end of his creation, so is not creation by any means, purposeless and on its own (Deism).

These truths and claims are all found in Genesis. Although not directly and explicitly taught, Genesis is rich in profound doctrinal matters of faith – the doctrine of God, creation, man, sin, redemption (as seen in the covenant setting and its development), marriage and human civilization etc., are precisely taught in this book. Genesis laid the foundation; the rest of the scriptures developed them.

A man who claims faith in God but knows not the doctrinal matters pertaining (to) his faith has forgotten he is a Christian.

Author

Nearly every person, including the greatest scholars of the Jews – Philo and Josephus, Mishnaic and Talmudic authorities, traditionally doubtlessly accepted Moses as the author of the whole Torah of which Genesis is part, but in connection to his death (Ex. 34:5). Serious attempt has been made by some relentless critics and scholars to reject the Mosaic authorship particularly, Genesis. Using the source tradition or documentary hypothesis, Graf-Welhausen and his followers attributed to many different authors who might have written it at different times and places, with different views of God and in different ways or styles of presentation. Moses therefore was seen as compiler of the work.

The basis of this argument is the use of different names for the creator, contradictions and divergences in outlook especially in the two creation accounts Genesis 1-2:1 and 2:5-24 respectively. But, can a faithful student of

Genesis suppose this to have proved the existence of different documents of traditions? He should not be faithful rather. Would these scholars could have read and understood Genesis as it is, but still result to this God-honoring scientific method of research? That we hold to this so-called theory is our ignorance of Genesis and its teaching on God, creation, redemption and eschatology.

Pointing to the use of different names for the creator, Genesis presents God at a more humbled level to a more glorified point of view. Nowhere is God's humility seen, marveled at and appreciated than in the revelation of himself in the creation and in the person of Jesus Christ, creation and redemption and, accordingly, nowhere is this honor and glorification worshipped and praised than in his resurrection and ascension and second advent (eschatology).

The name(s) and use of God's name(s) go straight to his personality as revealed at some certain times. *Elohim*, the Hebrew name for God, means the most high. This carries the thought of a transcendent being, suppernatural, strong and independent, whereas *Adonay* or *YHWH* for Lord means one who rules over everything.

That God was humbled at one time and honored at another is literally correct. This fact is settled in the use of God's names and descriptions. Take for example; John 1.1-14 logically depicts Jesus as God who humbled himself through incarnation, but Matthew 28:18-19 powerfully present Him as Lord – King, Ruler, and Governor of the whole creation (glorification). The witness of the apostle points to this fact (Acts 2:22-35, 36; 3:11-26). The teaching in Phil. 2:5-14 and most of the description in Revelation stands in agreement with this proposition.

The use of different names such as *Elohim, Adonai* or *YHWH* was therefore a sensitive and logical attempt of presenting the true quality of the creator, He is God and Lord. As God, He creates; as Lord, He rules and governs what he created. He becomes the King of His creation. So is He addressed *LordGod, YHWH – Elohim*. It is never pointing to different sources but to the true nature of God. Believe it or not it remains an eternal truth.

The Hebrew venerations of God and His name YHWH substantiates and proves the whole point. The fear of God is deeply and intrinsically rooted in Hebrews' view of God as King, and therefore powerfully controls worship (of

Him), life and practice. To pronounce and call the name in vain is as equal as sin of complete rebellion against God and should be punished by death.

The duplication and repetition of creation account that was taken for contradiction and owing to different sources is completely inconceivable. The first account states down what God creates (1-2-4) whereas the second, how he creates them and the reason and purpose of creating them (2:5-24). In the first account, we are told God created man and woman in His own image (1:36-38); we are told how he created them but in the second accounts (2:5-7; 18:24) man was made from dust of the ground and given the breath of God and the woman from the ribs of them.

The purpose of his creation was that man should be in divine fellowship with and service for (to) God (2:8-17). Accordingly, this divine union and service is to be extended to follow creatures (2:18-24). God has more in mind than just marital unions characterized by sex in this passage. He is revealing the mystery and meaning of life – that the meaning of life is not individualism (vs. 18), materialism and intellectualism (vs. 19-20) but communalism (vs. 21-24). What God has yoked together let no man put asunder. Sin is separation (from God and fellow being) and individualism. Men and women are created to live in unity (Psalm. 133, John 17). The beauty and blessing, progress and success of life is in unity. Divorcement of marriage occurs when men become individualistic in view and practice. God chose to reveal this purpose in terms of marriage union because the family is the basic unit of life. If the members of the family are united, so will the community, nation and the world be. Thus peace, progress and success secured.

In summary of the authorship argument, I therefore assert and confirm strongly, that Moses is the author of Genesis from chapter to chapter, although he might not have written the whole chapters of Deuteronomy, if it were taken chronologically. To deny this by the use of JEPD theory is complete ignorance of Genesis, self-delusion and an injustice to the whole Bible.

Let's know in conclusion, that the aim and purpose of Bible writers is not to marshal in an argument with the skeptics and critics, but to reveal the plain truth of life that will build the faith of believers and direct the course of their living and daily actions.

Automatic Creation

The difficulty of Genesis points to its first chapter. However, her difficulty is her glory that makes her distinct among many books of the Old Testament. Great thinkers (scientists), scholars and theologians are her friends and enemies for centuries. They found it fascinating and sometimes contradicting, yet couldn't leave it alone. But whether the difficulty is in views or approaches is controversial. Nevertheless, the understanding determines the approach.

There are many approaches to Genesis 1:1, among which is the *summary statement*. This is the most commonly and widely acceptable approach. By this approach, vs. 1 is a prologue and poem. The writer is concerned with creating specific emotional responses through the sound and rhythm of the verses; the writer wanted to formulate a concentrated imagination of God in the reader's mind, so much that he (the reader) has no option but to praise Him (God). The verse is therefore taken for temporal clause (prologue). Vs. 2 then states the condition that prompts the beginning of creation, the chaos, and so creation begins at vs. 3 when God imposes order on the chaos. Creation, according to this approach as Prenter Regin fearlessly puts it, is God's struggle against death in order that life may be preserved. Creation takes place as God overcomes the power of chaos, death and destruction. John Walton is also of this view. "Genesis," he said, "is interested in an organized world as against a chaotic world, and not in metaphysical question of something against nothing". Creation is depicted as the triumph of God over the sterile forces of chaos.

This suggests that the chaos proceeds the creation period. In other words, it co-existed with God as a free independent impersonal force and, as God wrestled with this force, the result was creation. For where should this chaos might have come from? Or otherwise, when God was creating the world, somehow, it got out of control and resulted in chaos? Of course, the common theory of good and evil appeals to these thoughts as the central reason why the world is as it is today. God can't control it, either because he is unable or he is not a good God. Creation was as a result of chaos, even as redemption a result of sin. God was never willing to create and redeem but forced by the restless force of chaos and sin.

The phrase *Heaven* and *Earth*, is viewed and taken for universe with a kind of some upper and lower region and because there is no Hebrew word for it, *S(h)amayim* was used instead.

Another approach is the one I may call the "Raw Material Approach." The African Bible Commentary accepts the *Summary Statement Approach* but in a new dimension. For this commentary, creation is not a single and instant grand of gesture but gradual work. In Vs. 1 God created the raw material and out of this raw material He created the world (vs. 3-13). The phrase *in the beginning* is translated as at first. To paraphrase, *at first God created the raw material for creation.* Vs. 2 is just the state of the raw material world. These then are two approaches and their interpretations of Genesis chapter one. Should they be right? Absolutely incorrect. Let's consider the first approach.

Firstly, the idea of creation out of God struggling with the principalities of chaos, which presupposes and implies co-existence with God, is in the first place incompatible with the whole Bible, blasphemous and inconceivable. The greatest fallacy and inefficacy of this approach is the idea of chaos independently struggling with God. Were God properly understood; then fell into these scandalous errors? Were we to be faithful to the meaning and use of our words; then still hold to this heinous thought? Is not the name God an enough point to nullify and condemn the whole approach forever? A sovereign being, supernaturally strong and independent, existed alone without any being beside or beneath Him but Himself, yet would struggle with finite untrue impersonal force? Then is God never God.

The cause? The danger of allegory and traditional idea of words. Take for example, the description in Vs. 2, taken for chaos and the dangers of parallel studies of scripture and of reading them in the light of Near East. For instance, Vs. 2 is taken in line with text of similar ideas and expressions. E.g. Job 6:18, 9:8, 12:24, 26:8-11, Isaiah 27:1, 34:11, 43:23, Jer. 4:23.

Secondly, unless we violate the linguistic principles of language, we have no right whatsoever to translate the phrase *the Heaven and the Earth* to mean *universe* or the *world*. The article *the* shows that heaven is real and distinct, so also the earth in addition or relation to the heaven. And if the writer was faithful to the linguistic principles, then Vs. 2 will be read, "And the heaven and the earth...." Not "and the earth....." But why should it be "heaven and earth" in Vs. 1 but the "earth" in Vs. 2? It is a deliberate omission or limited knowledge of grammar and usage? Perhaps is the question of meaning and usage. Are heaven and earth two different distinct related places or bodies that are seen as a compound word for universe? If so, does the "earth" alone convey the full meaning of universe taken for the compound word the "heavens and earth" as expressed in Vs. 1? To put it differently, can "earth" alone stand for "universe" which is taken for the compound word, "the heaven and the earth"? If universe refers to the upper and lower part of this planet, then by the use of the "earth" in Vs. 2, the writer was referring to the lower region only and so, he was not having in mind the complete sense of universe here (vs. 2).

Is the "heaven" in Vs. 1 the same with the "heaven" in Vs. 8, and the "earth" in Vs. 1 the same in Vs. 10? If so, then the writer contradicted himself. For the "heaven" in Vs. 8 and the "earth" in Vs. 10 are parts of the so-called chaotic earth as opposed to the upper region of the universe in Vs. 1. If not, then they should mean different things. Thus is the summary approach destroyed.

What is heaven? What is earth? And what is "the heaven and the earth" (in the context of the passage in chapter one?) We must confess that most scholars have altered and confused the terms for some expressions in the Bible e.g. Isa. 66:1, Ezra 1:26, which talk about "sluice gates" (windows) and so many other similar expressions for Hebrew imagery which are not a set of literal beliefs.

The Hebrew translation or word for the phrase *the heaven and earth is S(h)amayim and* for "heaven" as used in Vs. 8, is *Rakia* and for "earth" in Vs. 10, is *erets*. *S(h)amayim* can't be translated as *Raki'a or Erets* to mean the same thing. *Raki'a* refers only to that expanse, dome, firmament or sky as oppose to any idea of heaven as abode and throne of God; and *Erets* is used in Vs. 10 to mean only the dry ground (the terrestrial geography) as opposed to seas and oceans. Whatever the case, the use of *Raki'a* for "heaven", and *erets* for "land" or "ground", have a limited sense compare to *S(h)amayim*, and I suppose it the main reason the two terms were in the first two verse.

The idea of "Earth" in Vs. 2 has a limited sense compared to the heaven and Earth in Vs. 1, and has broader sense compared to *Erets* in Vs. 10. If the "Earth" in Vs. 2 is the same in Vs. 10, then the writer is presupposing the chaotic conditions to have taken place after the creation of *Erets* in Vs. 10. Then Vs. 2 also is a prologue, of which is incompatible. But if there were an already existing earth which is chaotic and of which out of this chaotic and confused earth created the dry ground called the earth in Vs. 10 then is our assertion true.

Moreover, if the heaven and the earth translated *S(h)amayim* in Hebrew taken to mean the universe, referring to the heaven in Vs. 8 and earth in Vs. 10 respectively, then is the whole idea of creation limited to our physical eyes. As far as this approach and interpretation is concerned, creation doesn't go beyond the physical realms. The spiritual being e.g. angels, in the spiritual realm are excluded. *Chechaikim* which is taken for heaven with reference to its extend which according to the Hebrews, the heaven is divided into three parts, vix, the atmosphere section, where clouds are found, the sky or firmament where sun, moon and stars are found and the upper heaven where God and his thrones are found, is not applied here. According to this interpretation, angels may not be part of creation. The heaven and the earth are limited to dry ground and the firmament where sun, moon and stars are found-period. When the Bible talks about heaven as an abode of God and His angels, it is referring to the sky. Also, when Jesus talks about going to heaven where His father is, he is thinking of going to the sun, moon and stars, so that Jesus is a special king of astronomy who ventures to make His home in the space. Stephen (Acts 7:55-56) and Paul (2 Corinthians 12:20) may be referring to the sky in their visions. The heaven and earth in Rev. 21 is meant another new sky and another new ground. Vs. 1 is taken as a summary statement, a prologue and temporal, and the phrase, *the heaven and the earth*, is taken for universe, then, of a truth, creation is limited to the physical realm, angels are excluded. But this is inconceivable. If creation involves angels and the idea of heaven extends to God and His angels, then the phrase can't be taken for universe. That is to say the heaven and the earth related to each other by the use of conjunction. Let me substantiate. Take for example, the Lord's Prayer in Mathew 6:10, "Your kingdom come, your will be done on earth as it is in heaven." Is Jesus referring to earth as dry ground as in Vs. 10 of Genesis 1 where plants and human beings live and heaven as sky (Gen. 1:8) where sun, moon and stars are found? He could mean so for the former, but the later? To be honest, the comparison eternally justifies that fact. Heaven and earth are separate different distinct places existed in relation to each another.

And if heaven is a place, then, a created place. The angels who are found in heaven are created beings. Therefore, the concept of creation should contain heaven and if so, (which is so) the idea of heaven as a created place in Gen. 1:1 is surely the same with the one in the Lord's Prayer. So that we can unhesitant and confidently conclude that, the heaven in Vs. 1 refers undoubtedly to spiritual realm, abode of God Himself and His angels although can't be seen and located, yet is real, distinct and experiential. Whether a place or state of being is both whereas, the earth as join with conjunction and refers to the physical realm, including the sky to the firmament called heaven in Vs. 8 where plants, animals and human beings including nonliving things are all found.

The distinctive features between the heaven and the earth are seen in the nature of the created beings and the states of life as existed in each. Heaven existed in a state of perfection, whereas the earth in a state of condition or process. Life in heaven is not characterized by (in the true sense of the words, not as taken for lust) eating and drinking, marrying and giving in marriage, planting and building, buying and selling but with joy, peace, and justice (Rom. 14:17, Matt. 22:29-30). Angels are not made up of flesh and blood, for which reason, they don't need air (oxygen), food, water, light, or dry ground to survive, but only human beings. They don't defecate; their sight is not based on reflecting light from the sun. They don't need to reproduce and their knowledge is innate.

Therefore, unlike human beings, they don't need plants and animals for food; they don't need air for respiration; they don't need the sun, the moon, and the stars for light and energy and for season and time; they don't need marriage or women for sex and reproduction; they don't need the dry ground for construction and cultivation of crops for food and business. This is the picture of life in heaven as portrayed in the Bible. But human beings, on the opposite hand, need these things for their survival and living, the very nature of their being demands for them. Life on earth was eternally planned to be conditional but not to remain conditional forever, nor should we attempt the errors of thinking that life is conditional on earth because of sin. So we greatly mistake the Bible. Before the entering of sin, man depends on the factors for his living (Gen. 1:26-2:5-24). Why did not the writer use the same phrase in Vs. 1, *the heaven and earth* in Vs. 2 but the "earth"? Should he have taken Vs. 1 for a poem? Then the whole setting of his writing, approach and style of presentation is contradictory, illegitimate and linguistically wrong.

The chief reason, and the only chief reason for that is because heaven existed in a state of perfection, is complete and intact. It doesn't need any further creative activity and arrangement to make it full and better, but the earth which needs an ongoing work of creation to make it complete. The writer therefore carefully, logically and deliberately ceases to refer to heaven again, because it is already completed and perfected.

Vs. 1 therefore, talks about automatic, an instant creation. God didn't take time to create. That there was a point in time when God created is true but, that he took time to create, even half a second, is completely unbelievable and pernicious. God directly created the heaven and the earth but the heaven in a state of perfection, and the earth, condition. In fact, it is only in this sense that we can profess the theological jargon *creatio ex nihilo*. If the earth was not already and automatically created, which earth is the writer referring to in Vs. 2 as chaotic and of which the dry ground (earth) in Vs. 10 was brought out of? The phrase *in the beginning*, of course, refers to time. But to think of time here as elapsing to giving day and night as in vs. 3-31 is confusing. That is to consequently think of eternity as day and night.

Chaos Or Original State Of Earth At Creation? Vs 2

The confusion in Vs. 2 has doubtlessly resulted to bad translation of the words in our Bible versions, and given rise to the Gap and Big Bang theories of creation. Therefore, there is need for great carefulness at this point.

The description in Vs. 2 is taken of a necessary, by most scholars to mean chaos. The reason for this is simple. It is the problem of confusion of dictionary. Is the writer here describing a chaos or original state of the earth? Are the words used in both Hebrew and English translations suggest any chaotic expression? Do the words imagine any formless and empty reality? Unless we are guilty of allegory, what is the writer's true intention in this expression, how do we know it? Is his intention to be sought in the meaning of the words of the expression in

Vs. 2, or should be taken in connection to Vs. 1 and, of course, the whole passage? In other words, if we take the meaning of the words of the expression on their own, what are they telling us, chaos? And if we take their meaning in light and relation to the writer's message and idea, what are they telling us, chaos? Do we have any right of taking Vs. 1 as a temporal clause only to read Vs. 2 on its own? How then are the first three verses related to one another? What is chaos?

The Hebrew word for chaos is *tohu* meaning an arid wilderness, desert, barren land. This word suggests nothing of confusion but literally explains the very nature and appearance of a region. If we paired it with *bohu* so that the translation now is *tohu wa bohu*, unless we figuratively interpret it, doesn't mean any empty, formless reality. It still just describes the state of appearance of something.

The problem is that we read this verse (the Vs. 2) in light of such expressions in Isa.27:1, 34:11, Jer. 4:23, Job 9:8, 26:8-11. But are not these expressions literal comparison and Hebrew imagery aim at showing her intensiveness, God's power and judgment of sin is? Do comparison and imagery mean of a necessary, that the two things compared are actually the same?

Suppose we think of a translation *tohu wa bohu* as a confused and formless reality and take Vs. 1 for a prologue and poem, so that creation begins at Vs. 3 when God imposed order, then the question is where did that empty formless reality come from, since creation began at Vs. 3? Did the chaos precede creation? Then it coexisted with God as free independent impersonal being or reality. Is this compatible to the biblical witness of God and creation (Psalm 90:1-2, Prov. 8:22-26, Isa. 40:52)? If so, then we are liars. If there was a force with which God struggled with to bring out this creation, then God is not God. He didn't freely and out of His self-will pleasure created the heaven and the earth. God wasn't willing to create, but because the chaos was threatening to him, he struggled with it and so, he triumphed. Creation is the resultant effect of God's war with chaos. But where is His free will, love, wisdom in the divine decree? Where is the place for eschatology? That a kind of such idea and similar event happens today in form of sin whose mystery can't be discovered shows that God hadn't conquered as happened at the creation, so in redemption and on it goes. But this is blasphemous.

If we believe and accept the Bible witness of God and creation that no free independent force, no not even chaos, existed with or apart from or that was above, beside or beneath Him, and no creature – living or nonliving precedes creation period except God, then what is Vs. 2 talking about, chaos or original state of the earth at creation? Dose the expression mean chaos to God or to us? Is God moved by anything outside or external to Him? Let us think again and consider our theology of God and creation well.

Do we believe in the testimony of the Bible? Do we also believe in the literal interpretation of it? Then let us extirpate away our erroneous preconceived ideas and presuppositions, our Near East mythology and inexegetible parallel studies of Bible comparison and Hebrew imagery, our allegoricalism and traditional meaning of words and accept ideas, meanings, and interpretations of the Holy Bible. The Bible can't contradict itself. What isn't true to, and in agreement with central truth about God is purely contradiction, anti-Bible, allegoricalism, rationalism, and confusion.

Vs. 2 simply describes (not reports!) the original or initial state of the automatically created earth in a state of condition, process or transition, that is, before the visible structure and living thing existed, this is how the earth was "without form, void and dark." The words simply mean "without structure, empty and without light(s)" respectively. We shouldn't think of darkness as something opposed to the truth which is light, as found in Johananine and Pauline theology. Before God, is nothing like that mentioned but in relation to man, not God!

The earth was without structure, at that point in time, God hadn't created the dry ground called the earth in Vs. 10. The mountains, rocks, hills, valleys, streams and the so called firmament, sky, done, vaults or expense called the heaven – all were not there at the state; it was void or empty because, plants, animals, and human beings who were blessed and commanded to multiply and fill the earth (Vs. 11-12, 22, 24, 28-30) were not brought into existence; it was dark because the sun, moon, and stars which were the primary sources of light and heat (energy) of earth (Vs. 14-18) were not created to place in the heaven (Vs. 8) yet.

The earth was initially watery. It was inherently made up of the waters, over which the Spirit of God moved or hovered. "And the Spirit of God moved or hovered upon the waters". This is a fact that no matter how high the earth may be, it can't reach unto God. God is always on top hovering upon it.

Process Creation: Creation Days – Vs. 3

Where does creation begin, at Vs. 1 or 3? We have seen and established that creation starts at Vs. 1. God, in a single grand gesture, without any interference and delay, created the heaven and the earth.

But what is God doing here at Vs. 3-31? Is He creating or He is forming, organizing and filling the formless and empty earth as described in Vs. 2? Or was the earth created perfect but got confused at some certain time (Gap theory) and God started to create it again (Vs. 3)? Then it's not creation but redemption. What is creation in actual sense? For some scientific scholars and theologians in particular, creation is evolution, a kind of progressive gradual development of matters for over long period of time. This view is taking directly in view of Vs. 3-31. But this doesn't stand true to the eternal fact express in theological jargon *creation ex nihilo*. What *creatio ex nihilo* is there when we can see the heaven (Vs. 8) and the earth (Vs. 10) brought out of waters and, the plants, animals and human beings, out of the ground or soil (Vs. 2:7)? Or should we appeal to the African Bible Commentary's view? Vs. 2 is seen as describing the state of the raw material and at Vs. 3-31 God started to create the world using the pre-existing or raw material already created. But this is surely inconceivable. It's still the same error of the former view – all are trying to support the evolutionary view of creation.

Creation, as seen in Vs. 1, I affirm again, is automatic. The earth was instantly created in Vs. 1 but existed in a state of condition therefore life on earth is also conditional. That is how God willingly made it to be.

Man is the chief and highest creation of God (Vs. 26-30). His life and living on earth is both conditional and transitional. He is not an aquatic being that he may live and survive in the abysmal waters. He depends on the air (oxygen) for respiration. So was the need for dome, sky or firmament called the heaven (Vs. 8); he depends on the lights; he needs the dry ground, called the earth for support, construction and cultivation of crops and vegetables; he needs the plants and animals for food (nutrition) (Vs. 29-30), not for companionship (2:19-20), so was the need for plants and animals. For continuity of life, he needs marriage, a woman for sex and reproduction, so was the need for woman (Vs. 27, 2:18-24); the alteration of day and night; one for his work, other for his rest.

I believed with Richard Lawrence in that regard, that "the earth was regarded in relation to man, and accordingly, each act of creation is the preparation of the earth for his abode. The work of each of creation has its specific application to the requirements and comforts of man and is recorded with that in view."

To be candid, God isn't creating in the actual sense of the term here. He is giving structure to and filling the formless and empty earth with living and nonliving things. In a sense, He is preparing a home or habitat for man. Unlike angels, man needs all the things created for his survival, service and progress.

That man is created within a limited boundary of time, is an eternal truth that he is a transitional being whether by death through sin or by obedience through divine rapture. His life is therefore, conditional until the time he shall attend his state of perfection like angels when there shall be no need of lights for energy and calendar, firmaments for division of the waters (space) for respiration; dry ground for agricultural cultivation of crops and vegetable, human services, plants and animals for food and social services; marriage for sex and reproduction. He shall have no need of these things whatsoever. God himself shall be his source of light and energy (Rev. 22:4-5); he shall have no need of plants and animals for food – for life in the kingdom of God is not characterized by eating and drinking (Rom. 14;17). The joy of the Lord shall be his good; no need of air for respiration but the Spirit of God; no need of dry ground, no need of marriage for sex and propagation (Mt. 22:29-30). Men and women shall be like angels. The word (heaven or sky in Vs. 8 and the earth, dry ground in Vs. 10) shall pass away to be seen no more because there shall be no need for them. Man has attended perfection. So the things of this world are unreal reality. This is our blessed hope. If we don't understand these things, then we are babes in our faith and, of course, I fear that many of us are still ignorant.

This is Biblical witness of creation and life. It is simple and believable.

O the deep things of God! Great are the teachings of God. Our minds can't conceive. Glory to God, forever! Amen!

Summing Up On The First Three Chapters

It might be, in case you could not follow in argument presented, may I beg for permission to summarize succinctly in clear and professional words of Albert M. Walters, a direct quote from his book, *Creation Regained*. I have highlighted written in capital letters areas I felt best explain my points.

We are all familiar with the majestic opening of that chapter (Gen. 1), 'In the beginning God created the heaven and earth,' and we realize (though it took a clash with pagan philosophy to find a precise theological formation) that these words refer to a creation ex nihilo, a creation out of nothing. The early church had to encounter certain heresies that claimed that God worked with eternal, preexistent, uncreated matter as his raw material, the way a human craftsman does, and the divine craftsman or Demiurge made the world in Plato's Timaeus. We do not always realize, however, that God's creative acts in the subsequent six days of creation do presuppose an already created earth,' unformed, empty, and dark, and the subsequent sovereign 'let there be's' of the creator establish a variety of creational distinctions (light/darkness, above/below the firmament, sea/dry land, etc.) within that already created but initially unfinished earthly realm. In other words, we cannot strictly speak of creation ex nihilo in the case of God's creative fiats in the six days. Instead, creation here in the six days) has the character of elaborating and completing the unformed state of earthly reality. This is what the theologians have called creation secunda, as distinct from the first and primordial creation of heaven and earth out of nothing, the creation prima.

We also note, in passing, that the scriptures here use both 'heaven' and 'earth' in broad and narrow sense. It is the broad sense that is meant in the opening statement that God created heaven and earth. The focus of the narrative then immediately turns to the earth ('now the *earth was formless and empty'), and heaven in that original sense (presumably heaven as the place of God's throne and home of the angels) is no longer spoken of. However, in going on to describe the divisions that God commands to take place within 'earth,' in the broad sense – what we might called 'earthly reality,' to avoid confusion – the story gives the name 'heaven' to the firmament as well (v. 8; cf. NIV), and the name 'earth' to the dry land as well (v. 10). 'Heaven,' then, can mean both the realms of God's throne and the angels, and also realm of sun, moon, and stars (the sky). And 'earth' can mean both earthly reality (in the sense of created cosmos outside of God's dwelling place) and the dry land as distinct from the seas. A second passing remark is that the expression 'formless and empty' in verse 2 DOES NOT DESCRIBE A CHAOS – that is the antithesis of cosmos (the currently prevalent interpretation, which draws on Babylonian parallel); rather, IT DESCRIBES THE FIRST STEP TOWARD THE ORDER OF THE EARTHLY COMOS, which is later filled in with color and detail, or like the bare frame of a house before it is finished and finished. The point is that there is NO*

DISTORTION OF GOD'S CREATION BEFORE MAN'S SIN. 'FORMLESS' MEANS 'UNFORMED,' NOT DEFORMED!

For our discussion of the 'word' in creation, this means that God's creative pronouncements – 'let there be light,' 'let there be a firmament,' and so on (eight times in all) – refer to creation secunda, the elaboration and furnishing of the earthly realm into a beautiful cosmos'.

If this claim is true – creation prima and creation secunda, of which it absolutely is, then shut we the mouths of the so-called literalists that creation actually lasted for six literal days. This is not only wrong in the light of creation prima but also blasphemous.. I cannot endure it than the early church could have embraced the heretics of their time.

As for me, whether the scientists are wrong on the date of creation, is up to the second and third party, but I know, even if they (the scientists) could be wrong, of which I'm not sure, they are not too far. That creation is 4.5, 5.8, 8.2 billion years ago is both true and false. It is true because it could be true. For who knows and can tell if it could have lasted that long? It is false because the Bible itself does not suggest or imply anything like that. But what are 4.5, 5.8, 8.2 billion years about but not another way of saying, creation, I mean creation prima, cannot be dated? For if creation is divine in its etymological sense, then it is a mystery, and if a mystery, then we cannot and will never tell the "when" and the "how" of creation. Unless we disbelieve this, creation prima cannot be dated. And if so (of which is not), then we have no right whatsoever to claim the theological jargon, creation ex nihilo.

It is obvious that Vs. 2 is just describing NOT reporting the state of creation prima, whereas Vs. 3-31 tells of creation secunda, God's work of filling, elaborating and furnishing the formless and empty world. Formless because there were no dry ground, mountains, horizons, valleys and sky; and empty because there were no plants and animals and human beings (to fill it). This is the only true meaning of the "formless" and "empty" in this context. Anything less or more is nothing but sheer allegoricalism.

Creatio secunda which was not creation in actual sense, is true, was literally brought up in six days. This is meaningful and God-honoring.

Creation Accounts

There is such thing as creation accounts. It simply means creation stories as recorded down in Gen. 1 & 2. Studies has revealed that there are two creation accounts, vix, Gen. 1:1-2:1-3 – first creation account and Gen. 2:4-25 – second creation account, and that these two accounts do not correspond with each other in terms of theological expression, style of writing and perhaps, theology! In the first account, man appears to have been created already but the second creation presents it as not already created. *God* was used throughout the first account but *Lord God* in the second account, etc. what is happening, contradiction or a myth? These are the issues that resulted to the formulation of the first and second account of creation. This discovery has being very wonderful in biblical scholarship in that it gave rise to the development of the Four Source Theory (JEDP) or Documentary Hypothesis, an argument against the Mosaic authorship of the Pentateuch. Others consider it sheer contradiction and have already given up on reading Gen. 1 & 2 if not the whole Gen. For them, Genesis is no less or more than a Near East myth. And so there is no point to wasting one's time only to explore only but an untrue interesting story. I'm neither interested in the Documentary Hypothesis nor do I consider the two accounts as contradictory. My position, let me put it bluntly, it is something of an apologist in this regard.

Truly I must confess, literally, there are apparent contradictions from a cursory study of the two accounts. Apart from the above mentioned, I can take more step to mention some. In day six, terrestrial animals were already created (Ch.1:24-25) but in Ch. 2:19-20, it appears the first time God was creating them. To make it more complex, first creation account mentions days but not so in the second. Moreover, it appears without argument that man – Adam was first created – the woman came out of him. To put it more simpler and clearer, the two guys in the light of the second account (Ch. 2:18-22) were not created at the same spot of time. The question is: How old was the man when the woman was created? As old as some hours, may be 24 hours? This does not only appear as contradicting the first account but also a valid argument against those who take the creation days literally. Until you can answer this question with a degree of certainty, you have no right whatsoever, to justify a literal seven days of creation.

I imagine some people thinking that I have succeeded in producing another new point of contradiction regarding the two accounts, but you may be mistaken. My reason and purpose for stating this is not to support JEDP theory but to identify with them in the apparent contradiction and tell them that though it appears so, yet it is not so. Whoever holds tenably to these apparent contradictions is just fooling himself. There is no such thing as contradiction in the two creation accounts.

But why and how have we fallen into this God-dishonoring and soul-destroying error of assuming the two accounts contradicts each other? There is but a simple answer here. It is because we miss the right stand-point of studying Genesis and the reason and purpose of writing the first two chapters of Genesis in particular.

I consent with Brueggerman Walter, that the right stand-point to studying Genesis is Exodus. Without Exodus, there is no Genesis. What I mean is that Exodus is the reason for Genesis. As Walter would say, every single generation that could last longer than a century must take up the task of educating her young ones very serious. God knows this and so he urges the Israelites to educate their children – to tell them (the young ones) their (Israelites) stories and narrate to them God's dealings with them (Ex. 12:26,13:8,14, Deut. 6:20-21, Josh. 4:6, 21, 6:6-7).

So you see, Genesis, and Genesis Ch. 1 & 2 in particular were written in answer to the questions of the younger and later generations of the Israelites.

I'm convinced that Genesis was not purposely written in defense of the true God and true account of creation as was confused by the Near East myths of creation, but also and primarily to answer the cultic questions on worship. If we ask why the Jews worship on Sabbath? You have no answer for this question whatsoever but by the first creation account. The Sabbath worship is the heart of Judaism. Remove it and Judaism is gone. The Sabbath worship has connection with creation order. In fact, this means that worship and creation are inseparable. But this is not my concern here. Ch. 1 of Genesis – the first creation account, focuses on answering this question on Sabbath worship, and it does so by stating in general what God did. And of course, the emphasis in the first creation account is on creation days – why? Why was the narrator careful to mentioning days? Because he wanted to tell why the Jews worship on Sabbath instead of Friday or any other day than the Sabbath. The reason why the Jews worship on Sabbath rather than any other day is because God fixed the word in six days and rested on the seventh, the Sabbath day – simple.

So accordingly, Ch. 2, the second creation account was written primarily to answer the questions of human suffering. Why do we suffer and die? Why is the world the way it is? Was it created like this? What went wrong? And how did it happen? I pity and sympathize with those who take an easy answer for these questions. But any honest biblical answer to the problem of human suffering (evil) and death must start from its root.

You cannot answer the questions faithfully without taking into account the details of the creation of man and woman, of the Garden of Eden, of the two trees of life and of the knowledge of good and evil in the midst of the Garden, of the commandment or warning of God to man. That is exactly what the second creation account does. It is NOT reporting a different account in contradiction of the first account but answering a question – a question of human evil. Anything less or more than this is an injustice to the interpreting of Genesis.

I agree with James McKeown when he observes that the second creation account **"introduces a more detail account of creation that focuses on human beings and their immediate environment."** The emphasis is on human beings and their state of being. But McKeown could not stop here. He went on: the two creation accounts **"give us two complementary portrayals ofcreation."**

Mark the word, **complementary NOT contradictory portrayals of creation.**

We could keep on with McKeown. The two creation accounts **"are not parallel accounts of creation."** They have a convergent point! But I'm interested in his last comment. The second creation account, he said, **"does not repeat everything that has happened in the first account, but it deals mainly with the details necessary to set the** *context* **for the Garden of Eden."** What an interesting comment! That is the point all. "It deals with the details necessary to set the context for the Garden of Eden" from which all the preceding of Genesis hanged on and are understood. Ch. 3 talks about the entering of evil into the world whereas Ch. 4-11 talks about the consequences of evil and finally Ch. 12-50, God's divine plan of salvation.

This then is the correct understanding and interpretation of the two creation accounts. If you assume they contradict each other as many Old Testament scholars have done so on account of the Documentary Hypothesis, for example, you are mistaken. You either recant your position or keep on contradicting yourself. God's words are never at odd with one another.

NOTES

Adeyemo, Takeumboh. *African Bible Commentary*. Michigan: Zondervan, 2006.

Burke, Derek. *Creation and Evolution*. Leicester, England: Inter-Varsity Press, 1985.

Carson, D.A. and others. *New Bible Commentary*. Leicester, England: Inter-Varsity Press, 2002.

Collins, John C. *Genesis 1-4*. New Jersey: P and R Publishing, 2006.

Furgerson, B. Sinclair. *New Dictionary of Theology*. England: 1988

McKeown, James. *Genesis*. Grand Rapids, Michigan: William B. Eerdmans Publishing Company, 2008.

Peacock, A.R. *Creation and the Word of Science*. Now York: Oxford University Press, 1979.

Prenter, Regin. *Creation and Redemption*. Philadelphia, 1967 Fortress Press

Richard O. Lawrence. *Expository Dictionary Bible Words*. Michigan, 1991.

Schwarz, Hans. *Creation.* Grand Rapids, Michigan: Wm. B. Eerdmans Co., 2002.

Waltan, H. John. *NIV Application Commentary* Michigan: Zondervan, 2001.

Wolters, M. Albert. *Creation Regained*. Grand Rapids, Michigan; Wm. B. Eerdmans Publishing Co, 1985.

Worthing, William Mark. *God, Creation, and Contemporary Physics*. Minneapolis: Fortress Press, 1979.

Young, J. Edward. *Studies in Genesis One*. New Jersey: P and R Publishing, 1964.

Youngblood, F. Ronald. *The Book of Genesis*. Grand Rapids, Michigan, 1991.

- **Spiritual Depression**

www.ingramcontent.com/pod-product-compliance
Lightning Source LLC
Chambersburg PA
CBHW052119070526
44584CB00017B/2563